A Needle Through the Camel's Eye

By Avril Bradley and published by Ginninderra Press
inter alia
The Fragile Geometry of Dancers (Pocket Poets)

Edited by Avril Bradley and published by Ginninderra Press
City of Stars: Love Poems for Frankston

Avril Bradley

A Needle Through the Camel's Eye

(mistakes in household management)

For John   Always for John

A Needle Through the Camel's Eye: (mistakes in household management)
ISBN 978 1 76041 XXX X
Copyright © text Avril Bradley 2018

First published 2018 by
GINNINDERRA PRESS
PO Box 3461 Port Adelaide 5015 Australia
www.ginninderrapress.com.au

Contents

1 People say...   7
'It is easier for a camel to go through the eye of a needle...9
Cleanliness is next to godliness   10
Cut your toenails on a Sunday...   11
Don't count your chickens before they're hatched   12
Sing before brekkie, cry before tea   13
Too much broth spoils the cooks   14
Eat More Greens   15
Pour oil on troubled waters   16
Everything's coming up roses   17

2 Home help   19
home help   21
Litany for Spring Cleaning   22
Domestic Goddess   24
House husband   25
Advice for cleaning women   26
Essential Grammar for a Cooking Course   27
Open for inspection   28
unlock   30

3 Objects around us breakdance...   31
a day in three objects   33
doormat   34
sink   35
toaster   36
Cutlery   38
Flop Drop Mop   39
Mixmaster   40
Jaffle Maker   41
Ironing Board   42

Mirror	43
bric-a-brac	44
chairs	45
Duvet	46
The Wardrobe	47
Garden Urn	49
hills hoist	50
Audience for the Moon	51
Wheelie Bins	52
4 Vacation	**55**
Abandoned House	57
Illumination	59
Circus for bored housekeepers	60
On not going to the Bungle Bungles	61
Beyond Blue	62
On a day you may have missed…	63
The House at Inverloch	64
Things to do in the belly of a whale	66
Starview Apartments	67
Old Postcard	68
Wish you were here	69
Rest au Rant	70
siesta	71
The view from a balcony in Noosa	72
Vacate	73
Acknowledgements	74

1

People say…

'It is easier for a camel to go through the eye of a needle, than for a rich man to enter into the kingdom of God' (Matthew 19:24)

To test this theory prepare both needle and camel before procedure.
Needle eyes, widely available, are too small for camels.
Have the eye of the needle custom made.
Choose a skinny camel. Anaesthetise it.
Do not use too much anaesthetic or the camel will be dead
weight. No amount of pushing will propel it through the needle's eye.
Expect snarling and gnashing of teeth (not just on the camel's part.)
Reversing the camel may prove a better option.
This has the advantage of deluding the creature
until it becomes aware of the painful pushing process
as its rear contacts the steel edges of the needle's eye.
Shit everywhere. A messy business. Not easy.

On the other hand, rich men are able to buy into anywhere and anything.
Even the presidency of an important country with a flotilla
of yachts, jet planes, automobiles, drones and a twitter account.
However the Kingdom of God is an unknown territory.
Unlike the needle, intangible. You must have faith in its existence.
Therefore access cannot be proved.

Cleanliness is next to godliness

Whoever thinks of God
next to cleanliness is wrong.
His Godliness has cleaners
to do for him.
When you meet God
he will not ask,
Have you swept the floor
or washed the dishes?

God did say, Let those without sin
throw the first stone.
He believes everyone is stained
to a certain degree.
So if you are dirty, no worries,
it doesn't matter to God.

Cut your toenails on a Sunday and make a friend of the devil

The devil never trims his toenails.
Have you seen the photos?
The ends of his toes turn into talons.
If he did snag one, well, yes I'm sure
he'd wait until Sunday, limping about,
suffering the pain before he repaired the break.
I still don't think he'd make a friend of me.

I'd have to do something extraordinary,
a truly wicked thing, before he'd notice me.
Like lick all the jam between
the biscuits Mam is keeping for Sunday tea
then stick them back together
and replace them carefully in the tin.
I'm sure then I'd be his friend.
Especially if I let him share the jam.

Don't count your chickens before they're hatched

My friend does.
His chickens don't hatch.

He counts his eggs.

His hen, Kitty
has laid her thousandth egg.

What an achievement!
One worth counting.

My friend shares
some eggs.
He shares ideas as well.

Some he keeps to himself
they remain nestled
in his heart
unable to be counted.

Sing before brekkie, cry before tea

I wish she wouldn't do that.
Tell me not to sing
at the top of my bald spot.

It's the shower that does it.
Water music like Handel
always taps into my throat.

I trill with skill
reach every note
well – almost

making music with glee.
When I had hair

she couldn't hear me.
No matter
if it were
before tea.
I never wept.

Shall I tell her it's a fast day?

Too much broth spoils the cooks

Everybody brought an ingredient for the bouillabaisse.
(i.e. the women, the men brought beer)
One wag suggested alcohol might pep up the taste.
He was withered with a shake of pepper. Belinda had no belief
in fish. She brought chicken. Someone reminded us, without fish
it isn't bouillabaisse. Marg, a vegan, insisted on two versions.
Bella bossed us and refused Donna's marmalade.
It isn't communal soup if someone is excluded, protested Eva.
Ivy presided mixing in her scent of sandalwood and
dangling red curls as she stirred. Marg heard a hare
had dropped in. She tipped the vegan pot onto the grass
weeping amongst it. A real broth of bother boiling over.

Eat More Greens

My father knew a lot about greens.
No one considered the worth
of the sprouts he grew from Brussels.
He was a greenkeeper, a curator.

No one considered his worth.
Home grown caterpillars did not mind.
He was a greenkeeper, a curator.
He decided to repaint his greenhouse.

Home-grown caterpillars did not mind
snacking on his foreign-grown greens.
When he decided to repaint his greenhouse
he forgot the price of paint.

Everyone snacking on his foreign greens
the sprouts he grew from Brussels
worth more than the price of paint.
My father knew a lot about greens,

Pour oil on troubled waters

Waves alloyed. Environmentalists annoyed.
No one now likes an oil slick.

Penguins, petrels, seals environmentalists even less.
Hefty fines will ensue if you dare

calm a stormy sea
like applying Brylcreem on unruly hair.

Spare a thought. Do you want a head
no comb can get through

or water where oars will stick
and boats keel over?

Best to let the storm run its course
and save the oil for salads.

Everything's coming up roses

although I planted peas.
The label fell off the packet.
I'm left with flowers like these

What can I do with roses?
They're not the chocolate type.
I can't cook and eat them.
I'll take them home to the wife

then when the days become like thorns
she'll remember I gave her flowers
forget her rampage and her scorn
and smile at me for hours and hours.

2

Home Help

home help

help your home
decide
what it wants to be

a cottage   villa
chalet by the sea
has it two minds
or three

do they come with a view
where the winds of credulity
blow through

let the outside in
the inside out

don't let angry colours invade
keep happy plants in the shade

Litany for Spring Cleaning

Let us prey   on the rebel rouser rattan fan
whirling like a dervish in a dust storm;
the dust that collects in crevices and on
the empty shelves in the larder.

Let us prey   on the nutribullet that burst
shedding its beneficence over
the wonder wok, the garlic grater and
his partner the onion peeler.

Let us prey   on the five years worth of
herbs and spices   used once;
the yoghurt maker curdled with
mould on the pumpkin slicer.

Let us prey   on the bathroom cabinet's rows of
precautious pills attendant upon
unmanifested ills and oozing
ointments uncapped.

Let us prey   on the free halogen lights
that splick   splick   splicker
blessing the broken neck
of the standard lamp.

Let us prey   on the stationary bike rusting
in the makeshift gym   going
nowhere with the heavy weights
used as doorstops.

But most of all
Let us prey   on the stale thoughts
                       clinging like wintry blasts
                       to the dying wattle
                       brought in to remember spring
                       now wilting in the vase.

Domestic Goddess

Hestia   domestic Goddess
the first to keep the home fires burning.
The first to survive domestic violence.
Swallowed by her father Cronus.
On the order of Zeus disgorged
born again to promote domestic bliss.
She never left her fixed abode.
Keeping the family together
preparing food and sacrificial offerings.
So lady, when you burn tonight's dinner
offer it up for Hestia's blessing.

Offer it up for Hestia's blessing
tonight's burnt dinner
a sacrificial offering prepared
to keep your family together.
Never leave your fixed abode.
Promote domestic bliss.
On the order of Zeus
do not swallow your children.
Survive domestic violence.
Keep the home fires burning
in honour of Hestia   domestic Goddess

House husband

Take the duster in your hand.
Finger it lightly.
Each feather is the antidote
to your testosterone-fuelled day.
Be kind and tender before
the dust bends to your will.

Indulge in some foreplay.
Music will help
the dust to succumb.
You will enjoy removing it.
Stack your complaints under
the Piedmont vase.
Multi-task as you hum around the room
husband yourself to the broom.

Advice for cleaning women

Remove the arms: ditto with legs.
Special attention is necessary for face, hair and head.
Contact a beautician, hairdresser, phrenologist instead.
Skin is the greatest asset. Do not steep.
If immersed too long chicken flesh will result.
Sponge the breasts. They may be flush.
Do not puncture with the nailbrush.
Crevices and orifices are awkward.

Yet thankfully, the vagina is self cleaning.
Pubic hairs can be removed by a Brazilian.
Get the nationality right. Do not use a Syrian.
Turnover. The shoulders, the back and the bottom,
places impossible to reach must not be forgotten.
When finished, study how to reattach the limbs.

Essential Grammar for a Cooking Course

Let conversations begin with butter.
Punctuate by rubbing into flour.
Knead in a verb to improve consistency.
Let the dough rise above the main clause.
Insert a colon before cooling off.
Take a phrase to adjust your apron.
The taste test will be a pronoun.
A whiff of anaphora softens pungency.

Begin another paragraph for the method.
Every good cook deserves an apostrophe.
Poh's kitchen is a fine example.
Hold the wine in parenthesis.
Too many adjectives spoil the broth.
Many nouns make light work.
After the comma, pause for breath.
Let every sentence end with a treble chef.

Open for inspection

Lacerate the skin of your dreams.
Step inside. See
the untouchable furniture
unused day after day.
Dust off the dried flowers
gathering a potpourri of
thought in the vestibule.
Rhythms of your voice
resound through interiors.
Piped music dulls
the gleam on *faux* marble
too new to wear a patina.
Unplugged nothing cooks
in the nightmare kitchen.
Hide your hunger
in the utensil jar.
Lift the dumb waiter to a
bedroom of unslept sheets.
Examine stale thought
as you unselve.

In the bathroom
the claw-foot bath grips
the floor like a tiger
wild for living.
No water flows from the tap.
Your feelings become transparent.
Ambitions rise, hopes flare,
celebrity fame flies
out on display.
The view from here
a lemon-scented breeze
of air freshener blowing through.

unlock

unlatched light
seeps through
night-tangled

day begins
in a spread of wings
thoughts rise

beyond clutch
grasping air
released in blue

a quick sliver
of an idea
loosens its grip

lurks in the passageway
promising gateways open out

3

**Objects around us breakdance
when we turn away
– Erika Meitner**

a day in three objects

knife

> morning
> in the street
> it's a piece of cake
> coloured SUVs parked
> misshapen smarties
> splotch the icing
> a siren slices traffic
> layers fall away
> the knife of it carves through

bed

> afternoon comes
> …and the bed dreams
> people upon it
> plaits the sheets
> in twists and turns
> creaks with the weight
> sunlight colludes

corkscrew

> evening smooths
> brings release
> the day's carping over
> the pull of duty done
> the corkscrew retired
> in the drawer
> enjoys obsolescence
> now the wine bottle is capped

doormat

beneath
the daily grind
the doormat lies
skew-whiff
a surgeon
too much on call
the blunt scalpel
unable to make
a clean swipe

discarded shoes
lie reckless like
crumpled mouths
their silence
thick as felt
under bare feet
the dirt tramps
merrily in

sink

tell her
listen
no interjection
no advice
down down
gurgle on
nothing sinks
completely
residue remains
tragedy trauma
joy ecstasy
passing through
drained

toaster

a creature came
crawling out of the toaster
a half-formed thing like a thought in the night
mountains of crumbs surmounted

crawling out
wary of distance yet to be travelled
mountains surmounted
surrendering itself to dangers

wary of distance travelled
ambushing the table with black and marmalade
surrendering to dangers
one sharp knife cuts through

ambushing the table with black and marmalade
the jug of water too steep to climb
one sharp knife cuts through
my hands faltering grasp

the jug of water
a plate of frozen daffodils in slow melt
my hands faltering grasp
too steep to climb

a plate of frozen daffodils in slow melt
water spills over the edge
the jug too steep
this is the night the river claims

water spilling over the edge
drips like a thought through the brain
night claims the river's surge
the moon emits a strange unsettled light

drips like a thought
throbbing nightmares wake
the moon emitting a strange unsettled light
falls from the edge of sky

throbbing nightmares wake
a half-formed thing like a thought in the night
falling from the edge of sky
a creature came

Cutlery

No charm
in your particular smarm and grease

Cutlery, you've served your purpose.

Now awry, you lie mutilated.
Smeared limbs sink
in scummed water.

Pans you have cooked it all.

Taken the measure of ingredients
        fried
                crisped, boiled
                      flambéd
done to a turn
                  emptied out
prepared feasts served on plates.
A festive array despoiled.
Scraps of gristle and bone remain.

After the civilities of supper
dainty china cups reveal
their true natures
        clink
                chip charge
                      crash

freedom fighters
faced with another immersion

Flop Drop Mop

Her retractable shaft, so long
        a one legged dancer
        she skims
around my room
        Zoom Broom!
leaping to ceilings and outer rims

she shakes her tousled hair
        dropping dreadlocks
        on my floor dusting
everything with powdered flair

She and I in perfect harmony until
        the clasp collapse
        reduced in size
her balletic leg gives way
        before my very eyes.

Mixmaster

I hear a blender sweating
        in an upstairs room
The pulp and mash perspires
        with every pound
as every limb goes round and round
        in the gym for exercise
And yet   serenity
        is what I crave
Not this forever
        whirring sound
The world concocts
Every body wants the ballyhoo
The perfect whole fruit of it

Jaffle Maker

I pack pleasure into you,
triple treats to make you burst
butter whispers, cheese kisses, tomato hugs.
Squeeze you soft until it hurts.

Press down. Close up.
Sideways dribbles ooze, retreat.
You can take no more,
sandwiched up between the heat.

I unplug. Lever up. Take you warm.
To your tasty innards add some mustard.
Savour every tongue-lick and bite
Leave you   unclean   burnt   and   crusted.

Ironing Board

We arrived at the hotel   depleted.
I requested a gin and tonic   he an ironing board.
He ironed out cares   ironed in pleats
on shirt fronts worried by travel.
Dashing away with the smoothing iron

I sipped my gin relishing the pleasurable
sensation of stumbling into memory.

Images from Elwood   surfaced in my glass.
Italian women   stringing
washing on balconies   flinging
chatter to the flats below
echoes multiplying the day's necessities.

No balcony for us. Not much furniture either.
We had versatility. The versatility of an ironing board.
Once a three-year old's birthday table
spattered with green icing   wiped
it became my writing desk   supplied
with sticky green ink   then

a clotheshorse dripping green-tinged wash
before two small boys upended it to sail
a stormy ocean of corridor.

My drink drained snippets of conversation from that time
collect in my glass   curl and coagulate there
furrowed wrinkles   never ironed out.

Mirror

Hair in a turban, a pinafore over her dress,
my mother glanced in the mirror and saw,
the curvaceous limbs of a Hollywood goddess.

Feet planted in sensible shoes, she wore for a while
not the garments of a housewife but
Grable's legs and Loren's smile.

She would pout her lips and pose before the glass.
Shift her stance, hoik her skirts and
wonder if her Max Factored face would pass

a screen test given by a famous producer
Goldwyn, Mayer or Hitchcock, perturbed
by thoughts, one of them might seduce her.

I caught her once, when home from school
she'd turned the mirror sideways
to practise pirouettes on the kitchen stool.

Dad came in from work, frisky and forlorn.
His wife steamed with cooking smells
turned her painted face. He did not scorn

but wiped the carmine from her lips,
clasped her in his greasy arms, then
smooched her with a Bogart kiss

and still today when wandering down our hall,
I recall my parents mirror dancing
like Bogey and Bacall.

bric-a-brac

sad cat salt shaker
still paws in glassy silence
live mouse skitters

                                        music box
                                        cobwebs dance in the breeze
                                        memory in tune

old perfume bottle
stopper poised sniffs the air
leftovers pervade

                                        snub-nosed venus
                                        eroded features wear
                                        verdigris stains

clay pig snuffles dust
brimful of obsolete coin
a noisy oink clinks

                                        blue man traversing
                                        the bent bridge forever
                                        china willows weep

chairs

in the night chairs   practise positions
imperceptibly   shift sturdy legs
               no one notices
the folding chair   slip her back to relax
the jason recliner   stretch out
the armchair   slouch in comfortable pose
cushions   grovel on the ground
the bentwood chair   straighten
the eames chair   pretend to be a throne
the pendulous rattan chair twist and twist again
only the bar stool   remains unmoved.

Duvet

You counter pain with gentle touch.
Enfold me up when I shed tears.
Your shape may not arouse
yet I trust you to be there for me.

To fold me up when I shed tears
after many lovers have been and gone.
I trust you to be there for me.
Cover my head to block out dread

after the last lover has been and gone.
You wear the weight of nightmare.
Smother me up to block out dread.
Protect me from the primal scream.

You wear the weight of nightmare.
Although your shape does not arouse
you protect me from the primal scream
and counter pain with gentle touch.

The Wardrobe

How many years, two, three?
And finally, I have the fortitude
to dismantle the margins,
the tangible accoutrements of your life,
expressions of our shared scenes, treasures
I keep to have something of you, still with me.

Your clothes are still
where you left them.

I open the wardrobe door.
You emerge in a grey waisted dress
a favourite until you were too wasted
to wear it. But now here you are smiling.
I take the hand you offer.
Kiss its sunburnt edge
before the flesh melts from bone
and you are gone.

In a dark recess, a heap of summer nothings
forget themselves, as you did in the end.
Crumpled now, I hold the bikini you wore
when we found that first beauty spot.

Then, I kissed its dark speculation.
Now, I tremble at the afterthought
of your sleep in the hot noonday sun.

The empty bag is heavy in my hand.
I steady by the wardrobe's rail.
Pluck the dark business suit
made shiny from the wear of work.

It slides easily from the hanger
no longer endowed with your will.
The last dust of determination falls on the floor.

Garden Urn

Show me a pot
that's not
in search of a plant
and that is where your ashes keep counsel.

Bright flowers surround
like wise words
your memory
enshrined,

splashed white,
after birds visit.
The early worm mourned
in rich brown earth

You were always one
for creature comforts:
soft beds turned down
potted wisdom.

hills hoist

sheets cocoon me
twist the clothes line
into a windcheater tree
the hills hoist elbows
a waning sun
pleats of darkness
shadow in
shirt tails
pale moon ascending
starches nightfall
with stiff stars.

Audience for the Moon

Laundered shirt tails dangle   bleached
by the moon's whitening powers on the Hill's hoist.

The floating boredom of a mirror nailed
to the shed door does   nothing
except
        reflect
                moonlight.

In the house   a vase.
        Withered flowers brighten at
              the moon's glance   bow

lighting cool pools in the table's smooth grooves.
Crumbs left over by tired ants   blanch.
A knife in the butter slices the moonlight
like a streak of sharp, grey cloud.
                High-backed chairs stand
                stiff to attention.
                The armchair slouches, slackens
                into comfortable pose. Basking
                in moon glow, cushions grovel.
The dark secretes itself in corners.
On the desk, business papers curl. Pay
the homage the moon expects.

A breeze lifts the loose flap of a shutter.
The shutter collapses, gives
a final clap for the moon.

Wheelie Bins

Weekly the bins drag us out.
The father and son animated after dinner.
Father's face scoured, smile fixed.
The son, chatty enough, his dead eyes shift
false cheeriness flung on the gravel path.

Last night though, screams startled
the house to nightmare waking.
The cold moon curdled.
The cat howled.

We do not talk about this.

The men promised us they would not die out there.
And now they are home and whole, so to speak.
Retired from the spit and polish of their days.

But can they remember how to be alive here?
Fix themselves again in this world?

In the bins, a noise
like the ringing, the ringing of each ignited shell.
Caution. Uncover with sweat and fear, the debris.
Look for wires.

There are none.

The I.E.D. turns out to be
as innocent as orange peel clinging
to beer bottles, bean cans, chicken bones,
cartons loosely flung, or neatly tied in plastic.

No body bags here.
No stink of bolt oil and burnt powder.
No injured mates to cart away
in Humvees.

Just trash, sorted, stored and stacked,
packed in wheeled conveyances.

Even here something always pokes through
the skin of things. Residue remains,
the stench lingering
on and on and on.

At the kerbside the bins are placed
to toe the line. To wait on parade
in uniform greenness,
coloured lids worn like regimental berets,
until the time comes
to be emptied out.

4

Vacation

Abandoned House

This house has time
        to play with itself
                now the bed shows
                      no trace

of those who have slept here,
        moved pillows, runkled sheets.
                Dust from rafters swirls
                      effervescent

like sherbet on a
        shaft of sunlight pleasuring
                its own reflection as it dances
                      on naked walls.

A strip of loose flashing
        dangles in a draught
                skittering stale crumbs
                      across the floor

where a discarded magazine
        dispenses advice, flaps
                to empty air with
                      wanton abandon.

Above the light flex swings
        as cracks in the plaster
                ceiling widen
                      uninhibited.

A feather drifts down ragged
        and docks against
                a chip of plaster
                        the shape of an eye.

A sun in ebb-light filters
        through dusty panes
                fades to silver softness
                        as the moonlight shift takes over

Illumination

I know why
> this kitchen moves its walls
> when the *bandoneon* plays.
> I am back in Buenos Aires ancient halls
> joining the dancers as my body sways.

I know what
> the caged bird feels
> above this squalid sink.
> I see loose limbs and flashing heels.
> Imprisoned here   I think

I know how
> you, my love, so faraway,
> keep walking in the grit of city's night
> as stars shine down from darkling grey.

I know why
> men grasped in poverty's grim fight
> pursue their dreams in tango dances
> after the barren hours of days without delight.

This is when
> dim hope spreads in fractured hearts, furtive glances
> beneath the glare of neon light
> a room full with tango dancers
> captivated by the music of the night.

Circus for bored housekeepers

Call in the clowns!
Open the Big Top of the laundry basket.
Roll up! Roll up dirty clothes to
tumble in the front-loader.
Let drying dresses ballet on the trapeze
and acrobatic dusters somersault with polish.

Montage cups on the dresser.
Juggle white plates with blue.
Harlequin hurl the throws.
Spill cutlery on the carpet to
bugle out the oompah tunes.
Grind the hips to salsa as you move.
Even though life abhors a vacuum,
twirl it, whirl it round the room.

On not going to the Bungle Bungles

I am a retail assistant in a department store
full of stale perfume and bargain hunters.
I could turn into the hidden checkout
secreted behind masses of discount merchandise.

I could be the elderly teenager who has been
searching for something unusual, most of his life.
I could be his palpable boredom,
his itchy fingers, his sneakered feet.

Here is the 50-year-old matron
who has never seen The Bungle Bungles
I could enter her cashmere coat
covering her silhouette like a soft sheep,

or become her svelte daughter
entranced by a bundle of leather belts.
I could be a pop star belting out muzak on and on
or the security guard – alert and alarmed.

But   I don't wannabee the life of anything
in this commercial enterprise.

I want to go to the Bungle Bungles
breathe in their red-centred mounds
listen to a quiet breeze
impart ancient wisdoms.
Echo my life in caves.
Be a bower bird surrounding
myself with treasures.
Coming home.

Beyond Blue

Days you lighten your heart, clouds clear slow.
I hold you like hope holds light.
We button our coats and walk the shore.
I don't care who sees my slanted smile

nor what wipes it away.
I hold you like light holds the hope
dark days will not return.
We belt our coats against the wind,

shield our eyes from slanted rays of sun.
Avoid the junk the storm has blown
into crevices between the dunes.
Skittered sand stings sharp our limbs

warmed by the walk, we loosen our coats.
Hope and light shine once more
We clear some junk the storm has blown.

I hold you like hope holds light
while waves swipe away, some junk remains.
I don't care who sees my slanted smile
on days when you lighten your heart.

On a day you may have missed…

the sky radiant since morning,
the wind dropped and
the bay smiled
full of flattened, shiny water
sucking quietly at the shore.

Visibility came in waves
through the stillness of heat.

The distant hill above my town quivered.

On the horizon the You Yangs bent
like camels adjusting their humps
in readiness to traverse the desert of sea
and move imperceptibly with the sun.

The House at Inverloch

after Penelope Shuttle

If ever we should meet again
and I don't see how we could.
It won't be in some closeted alleyway
close by the Minster in York,
where casement windows overhang
dimpled walls and you have to take
a Park and Ride to get there.

It can't be in a market in Marrakech
where moon-faced men jostle under
pure, blue lanterns strung up and bobbing
overhead – the gaudy display and
pungent smell of carpet dust
mingling with magic, Moroccan meatballs.

It won't be in the swoop of swallows
diving into the chateau at Chenonceaux,
the long sweep of sandy drive, green lawns
white turrets and shutters smacking of expense

or behind the black grille
of the cool courtyard in Old Seville,
fountain splashes soothing
the heated siesta.

If we should dance again,
it won't be back in student days
entranced by the vinyl spin of one song.
Peggy-Sue, all night long,

or in a crowded bar in King Street
loud music, gloom and sweaty bodies
sleazing in, then cooling off in Chinatown,
you spruiking your discounted words.

No, if we ever meet again
(and how can we?)
it must be in the holiday house at Inverloch
on a hot summer's afternoon
when my joy reached the roof
and left you behind.
This time, I'll take you with me.

Things to do in the belly of a whale

Imagine an earthquake. Listen to the rumble,
the pings and pongs of innards at their non-stop work.
Examine the passing parade of solids in slow dissolve.
Wonder who will be the next meal. Hope it isn't
David Attenborough without his camera or
the Biggest Loser with all his weight.
Think about Jonah but maintain the patience of Job.
Avoid ambergris. Do not blubber.
Contemplate the umbilicus from the other side.
Now you know whether whales have belly buttons,
store this knowledge in your head; it is the beginning
of your autobiography. You cannot record it.
Do not mourn the loss of your iPhone,
there is no signal in this cavernous body.
You can spout forth facts and shout loudly.
No one will hear. Enjoy the echoes.
Ponder the thought of entombed others, Tutankhamun
Jesus Christ, coal miners, at least you are afloat.
Believe in rescue. Miracles do happen. Rehearse
the memory of the outside world. Reverse your tracks.
Pity you forgot flippers to wade through fluid.
Exercise is necessary but do not make waves.
Count whalebones. Count your fingers and toes.
A sheer fluke you were swallowed whole.
Be grateful. Close your mouth and lie flat.

Starview Apartments

Welcome
You will be fine(d)
if you open a window.

If you lose your key
it cannot be replaced.

Your baggage is your responsibility.
Please keep it clean.

Accidents happen
but they are expensive.

Turn off the air conditioner.
If it gets hot there is a pool.

Do not hang on the balcony.
Clothes and towels are not permitted.

There is a surcharge for beds,
a corkage for bottles and a cakeage for cakes.

We wish you a peasant stay

Old Postcard

A past event
writes itself here
in stamped renewal

of a seaside holiday
lurid blue ocean
pale sky edges

long palm fringes
shading white sand
a sailboat bobbing

in remembered bliss,
I question this veracity
was it ever so?

The past and his broad
evasive brother the future
dissemble.

Yet in the present
I still murmur
'Wish you were here.'

Wish you were here

a poem in 4 postcards

i

I was in a quandary. Where to go next? I tossed
a coin and it landed on Innsbruck. I dropped it
down a crack. I caught the train. It was a euro.
                  bye for now.

ii

I'm on the edge of a reclaimed swamp. Imitation frogs
have been set to attract real ones. I told this guy
I write elegies. He said he had a lot of them. I think
one of them was on him now; he was sneezing a lot.
                  see you soon.

iii

I cycled through the Kröller-Müller sculpture park.
Wonderful paths with many trees and so lifelike. One
of them moved. Turned out to be the gardener.
                home soon.

iv

Last night in Paris, so I celebrated at a masked ball music hall.
Security was tight. Everyone had to show their faces.
One guy wouldn't let go of his backpack. They led him away.
                      Tell you more when I get home.

Rest au Rant

raised voices in crescendo
clatter on wooden floors
echo   echo   echo
scraped chairs screech
loud proclamations of
plates scoured
ping   ping   ping
phones ring burble ring
announce pierced lips
gobbled words drown
rinsed voices sing out
gulp food down
drink glug swallow
tattooed arms lean
menus make happen
muzak overall

siesta

afternoon composure
        undulating music
laps at the bedroom

in siesta's splayed languor
        pitch fluctuations
placate the heat

like cool, cool drifts
        the bedposts seem to bend
within arpeggios of light

each sound composed
        outside time in a space
furtive noises float
music captures
sleep's elusive note

The view from a balcony in Noosa

She has taken her old bones north
to wait out winter in a warmer clime.

Nestled on a balcony chair she writes,
eight postcards to friends left behind in wind and influenza.

Her voice – *such wonderful warmth* is light and airy, though
she counts eight instances of the word *ache*.

While the unit she rents takes air, she ties up loose ends,
dusts each one with the perfumed sadness of solitude.

In the jumble of memory, she forages for children lost.
Osteo. has touched her spine.

Too crippled to descend the beach stairs, she hovers
in the treetops burdening the sky, an old albatross

weighting the balcony with scuffed magazines,
a ruminant of conversations from vanished afternoons.

The sea allows a distant glance

where once everything was a dance hall decked out in scenes
       sweat, lights and cigarettes,
          harlequin colours of girls who weren't,
             their legs so broadly beautiful in the highest of heels.
             The diamond man with his *alouette*.

Someone is calling her between
banquets of eight courses and matching wines.

Her lunchtime meal arrives on wheels.
The young girl bends to clean.

Vacate

The air fills with tumultuous sounds
        Birds leave nests to frighten up the sky

Parachutes in the void

        Dawn expels the dark
Light obliterates the last cloud

Boats in the harbour bob to
        refugees fleeing bombed out homes

A failing shop of unfilled shelves
        Blank pages stare from writing books
Garages drive out cars
        into a commuter crawl

In the room your limp hand lets go
        the last breath cannot be held

Your soul empties out.

Acknowledgements

Grateful thanks are due to the editors of the following publications: 'Essential Grammar for a Cooking Course' and 'Audience for the moon', *The Mozzie* Vol. 23 issue 4, May/June 2015; 'Open for Inspection', *The Mozzie* Vol. 24 issue 7, September 2016, and *Valley Micropress* (NZ) Vol. 18 issue 10, 2015; 'Mixmaster', *The Mozzie* Vol. 24 issue 7, September 2016; 'The Wardrobe' was shortlisted for Cancer Council Awards 2012 and published in *Grieve Anthology*; Hunter Writers NSW, 2016; 'Wheelie Bins' was awarded 2nd prize in Scribes Writers Poetry Competition, 2015; 'Abandoned House', *The Mozzie* Vol. 24 issue 5, July 2015; 'Illumination', *Tango Australis,* February 2014; 'Circus for bored housekeepers' (under a different title), *A Lightness of Being*, Poetica Christi Press 2014; 'On not going to the Bungle Bungles', *Paradise Anthology* issue 3, 2010, and *inter alia*, Ginninderra Press, 2012; 'Beyond Blue', *Hope Whispers*, Poetica Christi Press, 2017; 'on a day you may have missed…' was the winner of The Editor's Choice award and appeared in *Poetry Matters* issue 26, March 2016; 'Things to do in the belly of a whale', *Imagination*, Poetica Christi Press, 2016; 'Old postcard', *The Mozzie* Vol. 17 issue 6, July 2009, and *inter alia*, Ginninderra Press, 2012; 'siesta', *The Mozzie* Vol. 24 issue 9, November 2016; 'The view from a balcony in Noosa' was highly commended in the M.P.U. International competition 2014 and winner of The Poetica Christi competition 2015, and published in *Imagination*, 2016 – it was republished in *Award Winning Australian Writing*, Melbourne Books, 2016.

Special thanks to Garth Madsen and John Jenkins for advice and guidance; to Claire Gaskin and Jordie Albiston for mentoring and workshops; and for constant encouragement from all my friends at MPU, Writers Block, Jenny Compton and Carrum Writers, Peninsula Poetica, The Yamala Bowling Club, Brenda and Stephen Matthews, and Pam and Richard Jarvis.

www.ingramcontent.com/pod-product-compliance
Lightning Source LLC
Chambersburg PA
CBHW062151100526
44589CB00014B/1790